The Scout Fire and Folk Song B

CW01621518

A collection of songs for use at camp fires and folk concerts

Compiled by:
Peter Brooks
Tony McSweeney
Brian Sims

Edited by:
Peter Brooks
T. A. Stringer

Cover picture by:
Bill Carden F.R.P.S.

The Scout Association,
Baden-Powell House,
Queen's Gate, London, SW7 5JS

Copyright © 1977

P. G. Brooks
A. McSweeney
B. J. Sims

ISBN 0 85165 126 7

First Edition
First Printing April 1977
Seventh Printing May 1989

Printed by THE KPC GROUP London and Ashford, Kent

Contents

Acknowledgement

We would like to express our thanks to the people listed below for the help they have given with the preparation of the music included in this book:

John Clements
Irene and Paul Garwood
Vic Jenner
Flavia Malim
T. A. Stringer

Introduction

For some time, The Scout Association has been aware of the need for a book that would help the leader who is new to running camp fires and folk events and which might also help the more experienced leader to add a little polish to his performance. There is a great deal that could be written on the subject; after all, camp fires have been going strong ever since the Founder's experimental camp on Brownsea Island in 1907 and there is a wealth of experience within the Scout Movement as well as a seemingly endless repertoire of songs. On the other hand, camp fire and folk singing is nothing if not a practical business and no amount of theoretical knowledge can make up for the experience of organising and seeing through your own successful evening. We have limited our advice, therefore, to what we hope is a helpful minimum in favour of including a wider range of programme items.

The rising popularity of folk music has had its influence on camp fires and has also led to modifications of the traditional idea, changing the venue from the evocative atmosphere of the camp fire circle to the acoustically more acceptable hall. This development is recognised by the inclusion of folk items as well as the more traditional favourites.

In the first section, we have dealt with the organisation of camp fires in what is really no more than a thumbnail sketch, warning against those errors of commission and omission that experience has shown to be inherent in these events. Section Two deals, in a parallel way, with folk events.

Common to both kinds of evening is the need for preparation. One of the easiest ways to guarantee that nothing will be overlooked is to draw up a list of items that have to be dealt with and then invite all the other helpers to add to it. It is unlikely that a number of people will all forget the same things!

Remember, too, that your audience has its own taste and repertoire. Most camp fire songs are fairly well known around the country, although there will be local favourites and sometimes peculiarly local songs. Folk music is quite often localised and even the more popular folk songs may not be known to an audience that does not engage in singing very often. Make up your programme, therefore, with the audience's taste and knowledge in mind, and include only one or two songs that will be new: your evening is not going to be a music class but a relaxed and enjoyable occasion and people relax best with material that is largely familiar to them.

Section One

Camp Fires

Camp fires have always been a part of camp life. Over the years, a great deal of expertise has been built up all over the world in events ranging from very small to very large fires. No two camp fires are ever the same; even if the programme were to be duplicated exactly, the audience would react differently to different items, now favouring the more raucous, now the quieter songs. The camp fire leader must be aware of the organic nature of the event, and must assess his audience within the first few items, being prepared to adjust the programme if there are early indications that the audience will not respond with the expected enthusiasm to what he has planned.

The evening's programme is, of course, the central and most important aspect of the preparation. But there are other, less exciting, things to consider which are hardly less significant. The fire itself must be carefully constructed and built so that it does not collapse in a heap after twenty minutes sending very hot, glowing embers in all directions. A properly constructed fire (we would recommend the 'pyramid' fire shown below) will fall in on itself as it burns through. Great care should be taken to use logs of roughly the same size on each layer or else the fire will become lopsided with the probable result that when the first log burns through and collapses the layer which is uneven will slide off and 'attack' the front row of your audience if they are sitting close enough. The emphasis, then, is on '*a properly constructed fire*'. Other types of fire, although possibly easier and quicker to build, can be more dangerous and should be avoided.

One attraction of the pyramid fire is that, with practice, you will be able to judge, to within five or ten minutes, how long your fire is going to last. This, of course, is very useful in these conservation conscious days when wood is at a premium, added to which it can be very effective if the fire is allowed to burn down as the evening draws to a close.

The size of your fire should be determined by the size of your audience; there is no point in having a massive fire if you have only a few people coming. The middle of the pyramid should be stuffed with plenty of tinder so that it will light easily. The next step is *not* to souse the whole fire in paraffin just before the audience walks in – it has a very noticable smell and is frequently regarded as cheating – but, some time before the fire is to be lit, to apply the paraffin, in *small* quantities, to several places, this will remove the embarrassment of the fire not lighting at all and also do away with the smell and 'cheating' problems.

The seating must be adequate in quantity and quality for the audience. Dignitaries who grace the evening with their presence might well have rather special seating, properly sited to give them a comfortable view of the proceedings. The prevailing wind must be taken into account for the sake of the whole audience who should not have to move once seated. From this point of view, they should neither be so close that, if the fire burns up, they will roast and if it burns down they will shiver. It is then that you will find that they will move about to the distraction of others and to the detriment of everybody's enjoyment. Comfort and cleanliness are also factors in these arrangements which you should regard as an investment in the success of the evening. Appoint someone to meet the guests and to conduct them to their seats. They should have been told what kind of terrain they will encounter so that they can dress appropriately and you might also suggest that they bring some extra clothing with them so that they can keep warm as the evening becomes cooler.

You may have your own traditional camp fire opening, but if not, try to have some kind of formal beginning, even if it consists of no more than a few words welcoming the guests and the audience. Once the evening has begun, move quickly into the first item and maintain the right pace throughout the evening. The audience must be involved in the proceedings and the leader should be at pains to create an atmosphere in which they all feel that they are playing a part and not merely spectating.

Most of the songs in the programme should be very well known to the whole audience, with only a very few new items added. It is not easy to follow words on a printed sheet by fire-light, so it should be possible for everyone to sing from memory. With new songs, the audience should learn by repetition, particularly through joining in a frequently repeated chorus.

Keep a balance in the programme, with some songs that can be sung with gusto followed by something that needs a more careful approach.

Rounds and part songs are very popular but they must be handled properly. It is certainly as well to practise beforehand if this is at all possible. Yells help to change the mood on occasions but, again, everybody must be sure of the words and the timing. If boys suggest stunts, find out in advance what the content is and encourage new stunts which the boys have written themselves. Yarns should be kept for strictly Troop fires and should be short and to the point so that the message will really strike home.

Apart from the programme itself, there are other factors which will make or mar the evening. Make sure that your assistants know what they have to do and when they have to do it. Encourage them to offer their own ideas and accept constructive criticism up to the time proceedings start. From then on, there must only be one leader if the evening is to be a success.

Control will have to be exercised. You can expect that most Scouts will be fairly well behaved but keep an eye open for the slightest sign of trouble. It must be stopped at the first conceivable moment. Insist, too, on absolute quiet when explaining an item. To keep things going, once should be enough for any kind of briefing. In the unlikely event of anyone introducing doubtful material into the programme stop the item at once and pass on, without any explanation, to the next. It may be that the audience were not as observant as you and, in any event, you will spare both the perpetrator and the audience from embarrassment. (Do not forget, however, to have a word with the culprit afterwards.)

Have someone stationed at the entrance to the camp fire circle who can look after late arrivals and enable them to come in without interrupting the proceedings. You should also know beforehand if anyone or any group has to leave early so that the programme can be arranged to accommodate their departure.

As for the leader's role in the musical aspect, you should be prepared to conduct even if you do no more than beating time. You will find, however, that it is quite easy to indicate to the audience when they should sing loudly or softly, when they should quicken their tempo and when to slow down. The more you conduct, the more important it is that everyone should be able to see you. When introducing a new song it is sometimes useful to indicate the notes, by the position of your hand, on a large imaginary scale but remember the audience is reading your signs the wrong way round, that means they will read from your right to your left, so you must remember to do the notes working from your right.

Pitch each song correctly so that the audience can reach the highest and lowest notes with comfort. If you should find that you have pitched it wrongly, start again.

As the leader, you will have to get each song started but it is a good idea not to sing more than is necessary. Rather, you should be noticing whether all parts of the audience are joining in and encouraging any people who are not.

When leading part-songs or rounds, stand in one place where everyone involved can see you. Moving round tends to confuse the singers.

It is unlikely that you will be using a microphone, but if it should happen that you need to use one try to limit its use to introductions and explanations. Do not on any account sing into it. You will soon find that you are giving a solo if you do, having drowned out the other voices completely. Test the microphone well before the evening begins; nobody wants to sit through that 'One Two Three testing' routine when they are expectantly awaiting the start of proceedings.

At the end of the evening, there are a number of things to bear in mind. If you have to make any announcements, make them before the last song. This will focus greater attention on what you have to say rather than talking to the backs of the audiences heads as they leave after the final song. Do not put the fire out too abruptly. If people want to linger it is because they have enjoyed themselves and they do not want to see the memorable evening being turned into a display of fire extinguishing. At the same time, nothing looks more forlorn than the morning ruins of last night's camp fire, so remove all traces before the new day begins.

Section Two

Folk Events

Folk evenings differ from camp fires in a number of important respects. Usually held indoors, they range from the Venture Scout or Ranger Guide session, easily accommodated in the Den, to the large scale concert aimed, perhaps, at fund raising, which calls for a hall that may well have to be hired.

Wherever the event takes place, check the acoustics first. Many a public hall is notorious for losing sound in the rafters, and the best time to find out is certainly not when the first guitar chord is struck. The ideal hall is one that is purpose-built for musical events, where amplification need be minimal, but there are not many such places to be found. Experiment with stage position; it is not always necessary to have the artistes performing at one end of the hall with an audience in rows in front of them; a central position or a position in the middle of one of the longer sides is often to be preferred and folk artistes will be used to being surrounded by their audience.

Try to make the audience as comfortable as possible, remembering that all public halls have strict fire regulations which require certain areas and aisles to be kept clear. If they are to sit on chairs, have enough for the expected number and let them know, perhaps by printing it on the tickets, if they are likely to need cushions.

Lighting is important, not only so that the artistes can be seen but also as an important contribution to atmosphere. Usually a couple of spotlights is sufficient. Beware the enthusiast who wants to experiment with moving coloured lights: they may be right for a disco evening but are definitely out for folk. Amplification also needs to be handled skilfully. Your audience will be sensitive to mood and saturation with sound will prevent rather than encourage participation. Position a responsible person at the most distant point in the hall so that you will get an early warning if hearing is going to be difficult.

Finding your folk artistes should not prove too difficult, the best method is to use local sources of information and also local artistes. Schools and colleges are likely to have folk clubs and once you have become involved you will soon begin to find out who's who in the local folk circles. Artistes will often perform free, but it is essential to find out beforehand if there is a fee to be met. Insist on paying expenses.

Publicity before the event is essential if you are going to have a full house. The standard methods are: posters, leaflets, advertisements in the local Press, Scouting and Guiding magazines, feature material (free!) in local papers, and mentions in information bulletins which may be published by Counties, Districts or Groups. Don't forget, too, that before any of these standard methods of communication were devised, people spread the word simply by passing on the information from one to another!

Selling tickets beforehand is useful in a number of ways. It brings in cash in advance which is necessary if you have bills to meet on the night and gives some idea of the size of the audience. But if your publicity has been up to the mark, you may expect a fair number of people to turn up to pay at the door. Allow a reasonable margin, in calculating the price of tickets, between just breaking even and gross profiteering. You want to make a profit, perhaps, and the cause may well be worthy, but uncommitted members of the public will not react kindly to paying through the nose for the privilege of sitting, possibly rather uncomfortably, and listening to untried local talent. The price on the ticket should bear some relation to the quality of the event; if you have a star, no matter how local the reputation may be, you may expect people to dig a little deeper in their pockets than they would for a night of community singing in which they themselves provide most of the entertainment. Add up all your expenses, known and estimated, allow a margin for contingencies, another for profit and divide the result by the number of seats available. This will show you the very minimum charge per head and you can make adjustments depending on the particular circumstances.

Programmes should be regarded as a bonus and you should be able to pay for the cost of printed programmes by advertisements from local tradesmen. Decide in good time whether you are going to have a raffle and if so obtain prizes and tickets.

Staffing for the evening needs careful consideration. Of course it is not possible to generalise but you will need some or all of the following:

Business Manager	to take charge of receipts and payments.
Catering Staff	to prepare refreshments and to sell them during the interval.
Compere	someone who knows a good deal about folk music. One of the artistes will almost certainly be happy to do this. The compere has a key position and can make or break the evening. He must be able to sense how things are going and to take the right action if they are not going well.
Box Office Staff	to sell tickets on the door.
Usher(ette)s	may be necessary to seat the audience.
Programme and ticket sellers	
Car parking staff	

The artistes will be glad to have a room where they can leave their belongings, prepare themselves and tune up. It should be lockable since they will not necessarily be able to take valuables, including money, on stage with them.

In consultation with the artistes, arrange the programme so that there is a balance between group and solo performers, songs which are known and unknown, items which are performed and those in which the audience will join. It is generally a good idea to start first and second halves with loud, join-in items as this will immediately create a favourable atmosphere, and to finish the first half with the same kind of item.

Sell refreshments only during the interval for consumption during the twenty to twenty-five minute break. Discourage people from taking back snacks to eat during the second half. One bag of crisps in an audience of a few hundred can be very distracting. The raffle, if one is held, should be drawn during the interval so that the performance is not interrupted.

Second halves are usually rather more relaxed than first halves, as everyone has adjusted to the circumstances. Plan to finish on a high note, leaving the audience with a feeling of having been involved in a successful event. If there is anything to say, an announcement or acknowledgement, the compere should say it before the last artiste's spot.

Settle up fees and expenses with the artistes as soon as the audience has left and, while you are engaged on this, your helpers should have made a start in clearing up to leave the hall as tidy as possible.

Section Three

The Songs

Openings

We have gathered here just a few of the hundreds of openings used up and down the country – they are just to give the new leader an idea of what to say.

Before pronouncing the fire open wait until everybody is seated, then walk slowly to the centre of the circle (unless the fire is there, of course!) and raise your arms until they are pointing towards the sky at about head height, wait till you have complete silence and everybody's attention then in a clear voice recite your opening – which you should have memorised beforehand.

1. The simple life and friendly cheer,
   May all those find who gather here.

2. As the flames point up so be our aims,
   As the red logs glow so be our endeavours,
   As the grey ash fades so be our errors,
   As the good fire warms the circle –
   So may our ideals warm the world.

3. As our music cheers us, so be the melody of our lives,
   As our mirth unites us, so be the harmony of our hearts,
   As our spirits rise to the lilt of our song, so may the
   Great Spirit uplift us to renewed endeavour,
   And may the happy fellowship of this circle go out
   into all the world.

4. Sweet is the Brotherhood to which we belong,
   And doubly sweet is the Brotherhood of song.

5. Here is an emblem, sparks that upward fly,
   So may our hearts be young and our spirits high.

6. Scouts of the world where e'er ye be,
   God shed His blessed light on thee,
   And crown thy good with brotherhood,
   From sea to shining sea.

Opening Songs

To get your production off to a flying start choose a loud, popular and well-known song – something to put people in the mood for singing.

If your opening song is not well-known or of the quiet variety you will have a terrible job to keep the thing moving during later items, so stick to the old favourites, it will be easier for you if you do.

Come on and sing with me

This is a very pleasant song which is easy to learn. It should be sung with a calypso-type beat and you can use as many verses as you can invent!

Chorus

Sing everybody sing, hey de roon oh,
Sing everybody sing, hey de roon oh,
Sing everybody sing, hey de roon oh,
Sing everybody sing, hey de roon oh.

2. Come on and clap with me, hey de roon oh.
3. Come on and dance with me, hey de roon oh.
4. Come on and shout with me, hey de roon oh.
5. Come on and laugh with me, hey de roon oh.

She'll be coming round the mountain

This popular and well known song is very good for getting your camp fire off to a good start. It needs little introduction, so go straight in with the chorus and start the clapping at the beginning of each chorus.

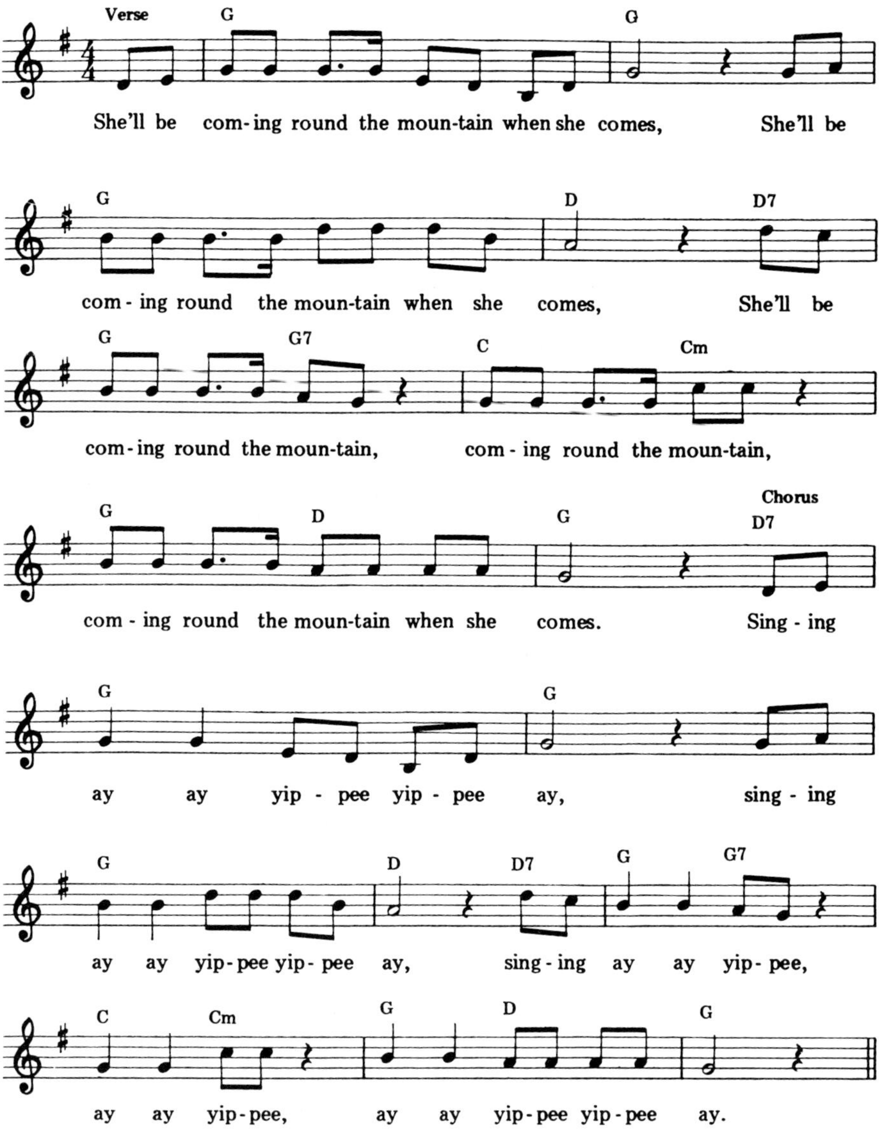

2. She'll be driving six white horses when she comes.

3. Oh, we'll all be there to meet her when she comes.

4. Oh, we'll have a celebration when she comes.

Although we have shown just four verses here there are many others, try making some up for yourself.

If you're happy and you know it

Another good opener, and fairly well known. The actions are simple: you just do what you sing!

2. If you're happy and you know it
   stamp your feet (*stamp, stamp*).

3. If you're happy and you know it
   touch your nose (*touch, touch*).

4. If you're happy and you know it
   do all three (*clap, clap; stamp, stamp; touch, touch*).

Action Songs

Action songs can be great fun – they just need careful explaining (you will probably need to demonstrate the actions at least twice) and properly controlled.

If you have a number of parents in your audience they will not be used to doing things of this sort but do not waste time explaining everything too much to them, when you have been through the actions twice start the song as normal and let them pick things up by watching others.

One finger, one thumb keep moving

2. Two fingers, one thumb keep moving,
   Two fingers, one thumb keep moving,
   Two fingers, one thumb keep moving,
   We'll all be merry and bright.

3. Two fingers, two thumbs keep moving . . .

4. Two fingers, two thumbs, one arm keep moving . . .

5. Two fingers, two thumbs, two arms keep moving . . .

6. Two fingers, two thumbs, two arms, one leg keep moving . . .

7. Two fingers, two thumbs, two arms, two legs keep moving . . .

8. Two fingers, two thumbs, two arms, two legs, stand up
   keep moving . . .

9. Two fingers, two thumbs, two arms, two legs, stand up,
   turn round keep moving . . .

10. Two fingers, two thumbs, two arms, two legs, stand up,
    turn round, sit down keep moving . . .

The Eskimo song

This is a well known action song and it is great fun, especially for younger singers. It is best to introduce each verse as you go along rather than try to teach the whole song at once. It goes like this:

Narrator

The Eskimos are a race of people who spend a lot of time hunting seals and as they set off, *paddling* their kayaks . . .

Paddling whenever this action is called for, it is represented by folding the arms and lowering alternately the left and right elbows to the beat of the music.

. . . they sing:

Chorus

Okki tokki umpah,
Okki tokki umpah,
Hey diddle, Hi diddle, Ho diddle Hey.
Okki tokki umpah,
Okki tokki umpah,
Hey diddle, Hi diddle, Ho diddle Hey.

Narrator
They look for seals and, shielding their eyes from the sun, they sing:
Looking to the left
Hey tokala mushuaki,
Looking to right
Hey tokala mushuaki,
Looking to left
Hey tokala mushuaki.

Narrator
Spotting some seals, they *paddle* toward them, singing:
Okki tokki umpah etc . . .

Narrator
When they reach the seals, they throw their harpoons and sing:
Hey tokala mushuaki – Ugh! (*as harpoon is thrown to the left*)
Hey tokala mushuaki – Ugh! (*as harpoon is thrown to the right*)
Hey tokala mushuaki – Ugh! (*as harpoon is thrown to the left*)

Narrator
They then *paddle* towards their catch, singing:
Okki tokki umpah etc . . .

Narrator
They then heave their catch aboard the kayak, singing:
Hey tokala mushuaki – Ugh! (*three times*)

Narrator
When the seal is on board, they turn for home, and *paddling* slowly and laboriously, because of the weight of the seal, they sing:
Okki tokki umpah etc . . .

Narrator
As they near home, they see their wives and loved ones waiting on the shore and they all wave to each other, but because they have been living on seal meat for so long they have begun to look like seals and their top teeth stick out over their bottom lips. With great difficulty, they sing as they *wave:*
The Wave: Eskimos wave by raising the right arm straight above the shoulder and then sharply lowering the hand to a horizontal position.
Hey tokala mushuaki (*Wave!*),
Hey tokala mushuaki (*Wave!*).

Narrator
And they *paddle* as fast as they can, singing :
Okki tokki umpah etc . . .

Oni wani wah ki wah wah

(pronounced on-ee wan-ee wah kee wah wah)

This action song can be great fun to do – and even funnier to watch. The actions are done in time with the music and although difficult to explain on paper are quite easy to demonstrate.

Actions

Fold your arms in front of you, move your right arm to point forward but still horizontal with the ground. Move your left arm and tap your right hand with your left hand. Bring your right hand back leaving your left hand out in front, then bring your left hand back to the folded position. Repeat, only starting with your left arm. Keep repeating this action; first the right arm then the left, and so on, and – with luck! – the verse should finish with the arms back in the starting position (this will need practice!). Allow a few seconds for your audience to untangle themselves and make sure they are all in the starting position.

Second verse

Put your right hand in the air and take hold of your left ear, then take hold of your nose with your left hand, on the count of three simply swop your hands round so that your left hand is now on your right ear and your right hand is holding your nose; simple really! Then just continue to swop for the remainder of the song.

Third verse

Start with your right hand on your right knee, your left hand on your left knee. For the first action, transfer both hands to the same knees of your left neighbour, then back to your own knees, then to those of your right neighbour. Continue to the end of the chorus.

Old MacDonald had a farm

This is an excellent song to get your audience warm and happy, but have a practice first yourself to make sure that you get the actions right!

Old MacDonald had a farm, ee-i, ee-i, o,
And on his farm he had some pigs, ee-i, ee-i, o,
Tall pigs, short pigs, short pigs, tall pigs,
Fat pigs, thin pigs, thin pigs, fat pigs,
Old MacDonald had a farm, ee-i, ee-i, o.

Actions

Everyone remains seated but use their hands to show the height and width of the animal concerned.

Old MacDonald had a farm, ee-i, ee-i, o,
And on his farm he had some chicks, ee-i, ee-i, o,
Tall chicks, short chicks, short chicks, tall chicks,
Fat chicks, thin chicks, thin chicks, fat chicks,
Tall pigs, short pigs, short pigs, tall pigs,
Fat pigs, thin pigs, thin pigs, fat pigs,
Old MacDonald had a farm, ee-i, ee-i, o.

If your audience manages to pick this up successfully you then just reverse the actions and there you have it – instant chaos!

Rounds and part songs

Rounds and part songs should be used sparingly, perhaps two but no more than three in any programme.

Decide how many sections you are going to use and make sure the audience knows where each section begins and ends, try picking out easily visible features, e.g. 'everybody on the left of the boy with the red ten-gallon hat' or 'everybody from the gangway to Mount Everest over here' (boy with tall conical white hat on).

Never use more than one leader and try not to move around too much. Indicate to each section precisely when they are supposed to start singing and when they must stop.

Oh, how lovely is the evening—3 part round

It's a long way to Tipperary* and Pack up your troubles**

These two songs are often used together. Be careful when bringing in the second song. 'Pack up your troubles' starts after 'It's a long way . . .'. Begin:

It's a long way . . .
      Pack up . . .

* *Reproduced by permission of B. Feldman & Co Ltd of 138/140 Charing Cross Road, London WC2H 0LD*
** *Reproduced by permission of Francis Day & Hunter Ltd of 138/140 Charing Cross Road, London WC2H 0LD*

Life is butter – 4 part round

Sometimes known as Life is but a melancholy flower. This four part round is sung to the tune of Frère Jacques.

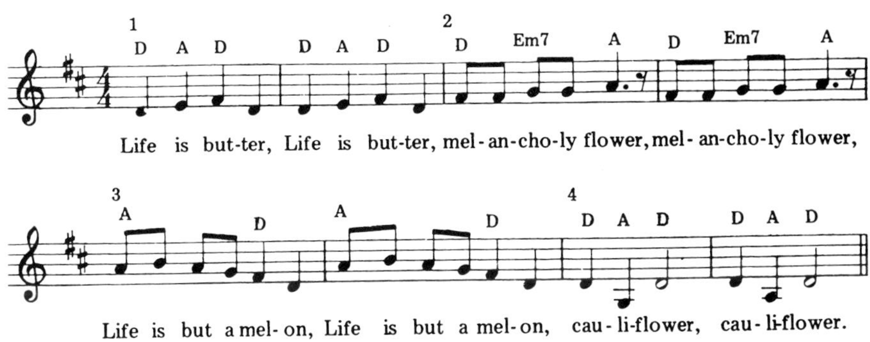

All things shall perish from under the sky – 3 part round

This is another simple little song, but this time in three parts.

Make new friends – 2 or 4 part round

This easy to learn round can be sung by two or four parts.

Yells

Yells should be done well, or not at all – this may sound rather harsh but it is true.

As with the action songs, run through the words twice before embarking on 'the real thing'.

The frog and the steamroller

For this very popular yell we owe thanks to Sid Taylor of Gilwell.

Split the camp fire into two parts, the first half to be the steamrollers, the second half to be the frogs.

The steamrollers make a noise like:
Sssshhhhhhhhhhhhhhh!

The frogs make a noise like a piece of wet fish dropping on to a piece of marble.

The story you use is as follows:
There is a long, long road and at one end is a great big steamroller, at the other end is a big fat frog. These two gradually make their way towards each other – you slowly bring in each side, alternately making their noises, then gradually build up the pace as they get nearer and nearer until they meet in the middle and everyone gives a loud squelching noise.

I say, have you heard about Hairy?

For this action yell from America the audience should all be standing.

**I say, have you heard about Hairy?
He's just got back from the front,
Where he was needed at the foot of the Army,
Everyone knows about Hairy.
Three cheers:
Hooray,
Hooray,
Hooray.**

Actions:
Very simple – just touch the parts of the body (your own) as they are mentioned, i.e.
I . . . say . . . heard . . . Hairy.

There ain't no flies on us

Another two part yell which can be thrown into the programme at any time.

**1st half : There ain't no flies on us,
2nd half : There ain't no flies on us,
1st half : There may be flies on some of you guys,
2nd half : But there ain't no flies on us.**

Ham and Eggs

The best effects on this yell are achieved when the whole audience is shouting as loud as they can.

1st side	*2nd side*
Ham and eggs	**Ham and eggs**
I like mine done nice and brown	**I like mine done upside down**
Flip 'em	**Flop 'em**
Flip 'em	**Flop 'em**
(together)	
Ham and eggs	**Ham and eggs**

Quiet Songs

Try varying the pace of your songs occasionally, after you have started off at a fast pace use two or three more of similar pace then build the pace up again. If you choose the right song for your quiet spot it can have a very pronounced effect on your audience.

As the fire begins to die down slow the pace down again so that you will finish on a quiet, thoughtful note.

He's got the whole world in His hands

2. He's got the little biddy baby in His hands,
   He's got the little biddy baby in His hands,
   He's got the little biddy baby in His hands,
   He's got the whole world in His hands.

Repeat first verse as chorus.

3. He's got the sun and the moon in His hands.

4. He's got you and me, brother, in His hands.

5. He's got my father and my mother in His hands.

6. He's got my sister and my brother in His hands.

The audience clapping quietly during this song can be very effective providing it does not get too loud.

Hush little baby

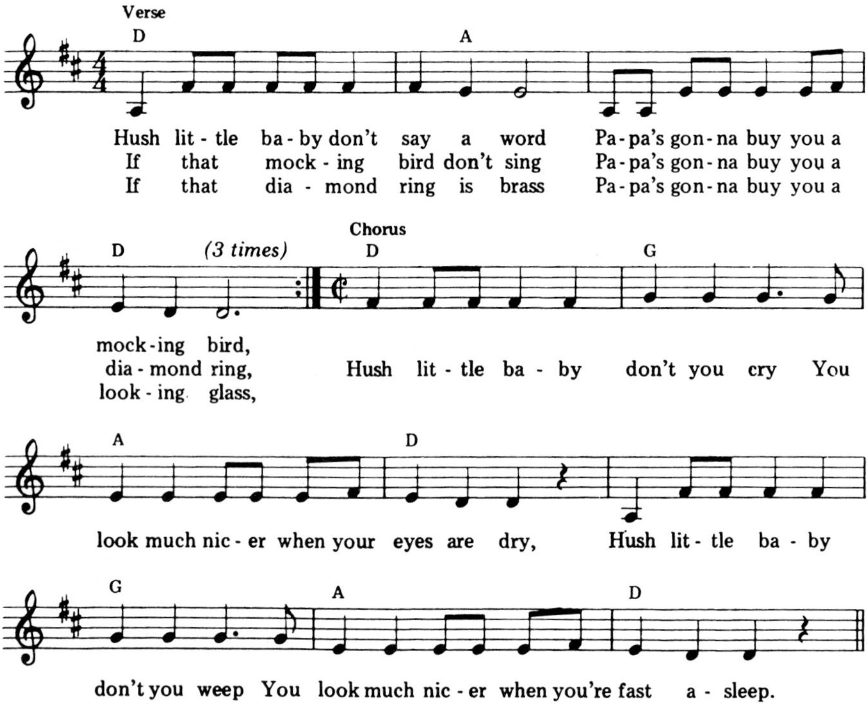

1. Hush little baby don't say a word, Papa's gonna buy you a mocking bird,
   If that mocking bird don't sing, Papa's gonna buy you a diamond ring,
   If that diamond ring is brass, Papa's gonna buy you a looking glass.

Chorus

Hush little baby don't you cry, you look much nicer when your eyes are dry.
Hush little baby don't you weep, you look much nicer when you're fast asleep.

2. If that looking glass gets broke, Papa's gonna buy you a billy goat,
   If that billy goat won't pull, Papa's gonna buy you a cart and bull,
   If that cart and bull turn over, Papa's gonna buy you a dog named Rover.

3. If that dog named Rover won't bark, Papa's gonna buy you a horse and cart.
   If that horse and cart fall down, you'll still be the sweetest little baby in town.

Go, tell it on the mountain

2. And lo, when they had seen it,
   They all bowed down and prayed,
   They travelled on together,
   To where the babe was laid.

3. When I was a seeker,
   I sought both night and day,
   I asked my Lord to help me,
   And He showed me the way.

4. He made me a watchman,
   Upon the city wall,
   And if I am a Christian,
   I am the least of all.

Standin' in the need of prayer

The first and third lines of this should be sung by a solo voice, the second and fourth lines and the chorus are the response by the whole audience.

2. Not my mother, not my father, but it's me, O Lord.
3. Not the preacher, not the deacon, but it's me, O Lord.
4. Not the teacher, not the doctor, but it's me, O Lord.
5. Not my friends or my relations, but it's me, O Lord.

Repeat chorus twice to finish.

Ezekiel's wheel

2. Ezekiel saw a flame a-burning,
   Way in the middle of the air,
   A flame within a flame a-burning,
   Way in the middle of the air,
   And the little flame burned by faith,
   And the big flame burned by the grace of God,
   Ezekiel saw a flame a-burning,
   Way in the middle of the air.

I'm gonna walk and talk with Jesus

Verses

1. I'm gonna tell God how you treat me,
   I'm gonna tell God how you treat me one of these days, hallelujah,
   I'm gonna tell God how you treat me,
   Gonna tell God how you treat me one of these days.
2. I'm gonna read the Holy Bible,
3. I'm gonna meet my Lord and Saviour,
4. I'm gonna sing some of them good songs,
5. I'm gonna walk along life's hard road,
6. I'm gonna reach for the highest mountain,
7. I'm gonna pray for all my brothers,
8. I'm gonna shout Glory! Glory!

Oh, Mary don't you weep

Verses

1. Who's those children all dressed in red,
   Who's those children all dressed in red,
   They are the children that Moses led,
   Oh Mary don't you weep.

2. Who's those children all dressed in blue,
   Who's those children all dressed in blue,
   They are the children that Moses led through,
   Oh Mary don't you weep.

3. Who's those children all dressed in black . . .
   They are the children that won't come back . . .

4. Who's those children all dressed in white . . .
   They are the children of the Israelite . . .

Repeat chorus twice to finish.

Rosen fra Fünn

The words mean: 'Roses from Fünn', Fünn being a part of Denmark.

We're on the Scouting trail

This really good Scouting song is excellent for bringing the tempo down as you approach the close of the evening.

This can also be sung as a two-part round using the same words. The second half should be brought in when the first half has reached the first 'trail'. Just because it is being sung as a round, it does not mean that it should be sung any louder than normal.

The gipsy rover

2. She left her father's castle gates,
   She left her own fond lover,
   She left her servants and her state,
   To follow the gipsy rover.

3. Her father saddled up his fastest steed,
   Roamed the valleys all over,
   Sought his daughter at great speed,
   And the whistling gipsy rover.

4. He came at last to a mansion fine,
   Down by the River Plady,
   And there was music and there was wine,
   For the gipsy and his lady.

5. 'He is no gipsy, my father', she cried,
   'But lord of these lands all over,
   And I will stay till my dying day,
   With my whistling gipsy rover.'

General Songs

For the bulk of your programme.

This section, as it has to fill about 75 per cent of your programme, has, of necessity, to be the largest section.

These songs cover all manner of subjects, moods and tastes. They are in no particular order and most apply equally well to either folk event or camp fire.

Choose your material carefully – you should have the majority of songs that are known by nearly everybody, do not include more than two or three new songs as teaching them takes time and if you spend too long on this the audience's attention will waver and you will have a hard job regaining it.

On Ilkley Moor bah't 'at

2. Thar's goin' t' catch thou death o' cauld,
   Death o' cauld,
   On Ilkley Moor bah't 'at,
   Thar's goin' t' catch thou death o' cauld,
   Thar's goin' t' catch thou death o' cauld.

3. Then we shall 'ave to bury thee,

4. Then t'warms 'll cum an' eat thee up.

5. Then ducks'll cum an' eat up t'warms.

6. Then we shall cum an' eat up ducks.

7. Then we shall 'ave eaten thee.

The Keeper

The keep - er did a hunt - ing go and
un-der his cloak he car-ried a bow, All for to shoot at a
mer-ry lit - tle doe A - mong the leaves so___ green - o.
Chorus
Jack - ie Boy, Mas - ter, Sing ye well, Ve - ry well, Hey down, Hoe down,
der - ry der - ry down, A - mong the leaves so___ green - o, To my
hey down down, To my hoe down down, Hey down, Hoe down,
der - ry der - ry down, A - mong the leaves so___ green - o.

Chorus

The audience should be split into two sections, one half sings the first line of A and the second half replies with the first line of B, then back to A and so on.

	A	B
	Jackie boy?	Master!
	Sing ye well?	Very well!
	Hey down!	Hoe down!
All:	Derry, derry down, among the leaves so green-o,	
	To my hey, down, down,	To my hoe, down, down,
	Hey down!	Hoe down!
All:	Derry, derry down, among the leaves so green-o.	

2. The first doe he shot at, he missed,
The second doe he trimmed, he kissed,
The third doe went where nobody missed,
Among the leaves so green-o.

3. The fourth doe she got caught by a tree,
Because of this she could not flee,
So he slew her quite leisurely,
Among the leaves so green-o.

4. The fifth doe she did cross the brook,
The keeper brought her back with his crook,
Where she is now you must go and look,
Among the leaves so green-o.

Tavern in the town

2. He left me for a damsel dark, damsel dark,
   And every night they used to spark, used to spark,
   And now my love, once true to me,
   Takes that dark damsel on his knee.

3. Oh, dig my grave both wide and deep, wide and deep,
   Put tomb-stones at my head and feet, head and feet,
   And on my breast carve a turtle dove,
   To signify I died of love.

The corporation muck cart

This song is dedicated to the gentlemen who, in olden times, went round on their horse drawn carts emptying the drains with long handled ladles. It should be sung to the tune of 'There's no place like home'.

The Great American Railway

2. In eighteen hundred and sixty two,
I found myself with little to do,
I found myself with little to do,
Beside the American Railway.

3. In eighteen hundred and sixty three,
The railway boss accepted me . . .
To work upon the Railway.

4. In eighteen hundred and sixty four,
My hands and feet were awful sore . . .
From working on the Railway.

5. In eighteen hundred and sixty five,
I was more dead than alive . . .
From working on the Railway.

6. In eighteen hundred and sixty six,
I stepped upon some dynamite sticks . . .
Whilst working upon the Railway.

7. In eighteen hundred and sixty seven,
I found myself on the way to heaven . . .
Above the American Railway.

8. In eighteen hundred and sixty eight,
I was knocking on the Golden Gate . . .
Above the American Railway.

9. In eighteen hundred and sixty nine,
A set of wings and a harp were mine . . .
Way over the American Railway.

10. In eighteen hundred and sixty ten,
If you want any more you can sing it again . . .
The Great American Railway.

Wild rover

xxxx = claps

2. I went to an ale-house I used to frequent,
   And told the landlady my money was spent,
   I asked her for credit, she answered me 'Nay',
   'Sure it's custom like yours I can have anyday'.

3. Then out of my pocket I drew sovereigns bright,
   And the landlady's eyes opened wide with delight,
   She said 'I have whiskey and wines of the best,
   And those words I've just spoken were only in jest'.

4. I'll go home to my parents, confess what I've done,
   And I'll ask them to pardon their prodigal son,
   And if they forgive me as oft times before,
   I never will play the wild rover no more.

Oh, the Johnson boys

This song is fairly well known but it is still worthy of inclusion.

To vary it slightly for the second verse keep the 'Oh' going for as long as you like, then when you sing it a third time alter it again – it can be quite fun.

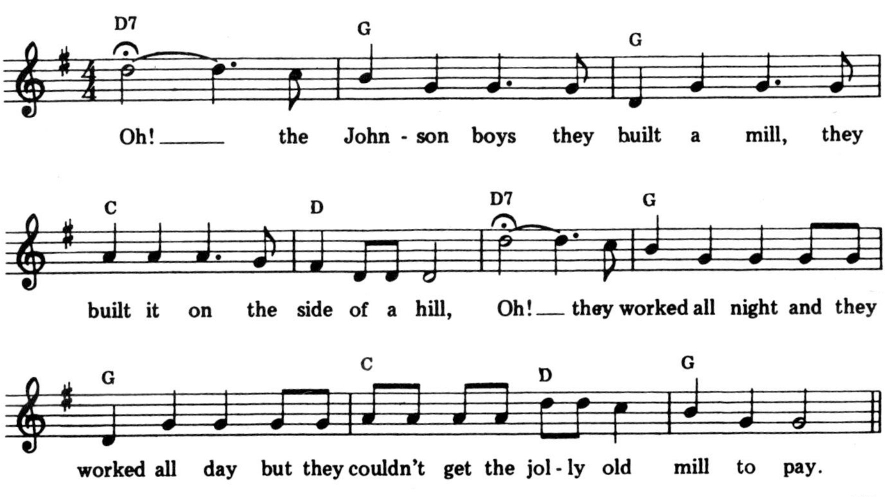

This train (is bound for glory)

2. This train don't carry no gamblers, this train,
   This train don't carry no gamblers, this train,
   This train don't carry no gamblers,
   No hypocrites, no midnight ramblers,
   This train is bound for glory, this train.

3. This train is bound for speed now, this train,
   Fastest train you ever did see now.

4. This train don't carry no rustlers, this train,
   Side-street-walkers or two bit hustlers.

5. This train is solid black now this train,
   Where it carry you, you don't come back now.

6. This train don't carry white or black, this train,
   Everybody ride it is treated alike now.

Be kind to your web-footed friends

This song, which is sung to the tune of 'Stars and Stripes', needs careful controlling because it can easily get out of hand.

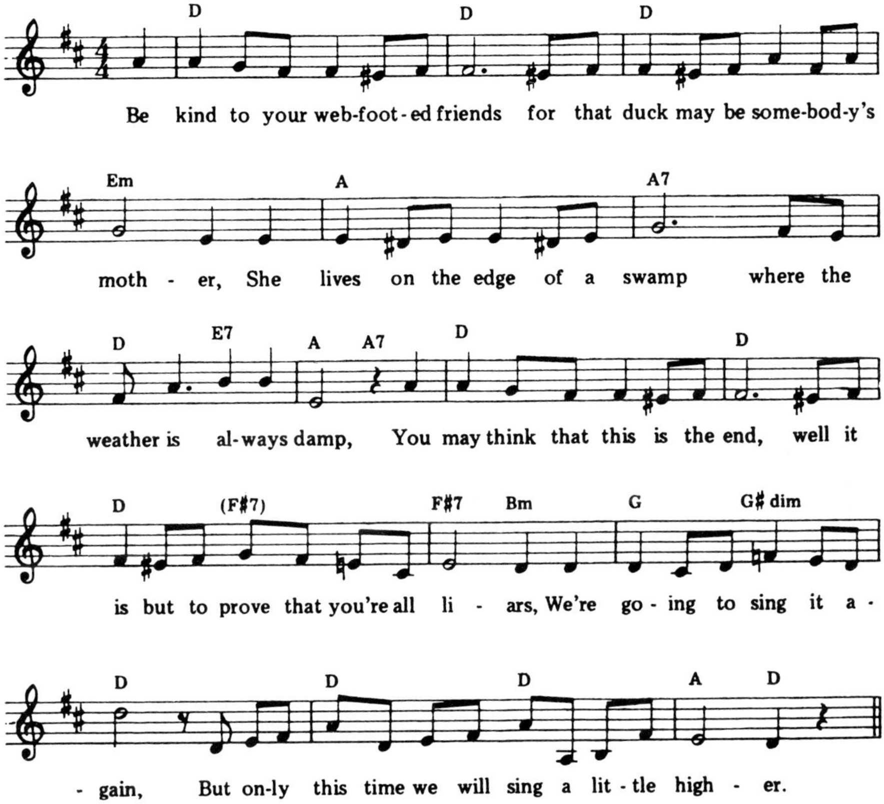

Repeat this verse but singing, as the song says, a little higher. We suggest that you continue this for two or at most three more verses.

A-Roving

2. Her eyes were like two stars so bright,
   Mark well what I do say,
   Her eyes were like two stars so bright,
   Her face was fair, her step was light,
   I'll go no more a-roving with you fair maid.

3. Her cheeks were like the rosebuds red . . .
   There's a wealth of hair upon her head . . .

4. And if you'd know this maiden's name . . .
   Why, soon mine 't'will be the same . . .

Mama don't allow....

2. Mama don't allow no camp fire singing here . . .
   I'll keep on singing anyhow . . .

3. Mama don't allow no banjo picking here . . .
   I'll pick my banjo anyhow . . .

4. Mama don't allow no folk songs here . . .
   I'll sings those folk songs anyhow . . .

5. Mama don't allow no tent pitching here . . .
   I'll pitch my tent anyhow . . .

6. Mama don't allow no jazz band playing here . . .
   We'll play that jazz music anyhow . . .

Reproduced by permission of Campbell Connelly & Co. Ltd., of Denmark Street, London WC2.

Take this hammer

2. If he asks you, yeh, was I running, yeh,
   If he asks you, yeh, was I running, yeh,
   If he asks you, yeh, was I running, yeh,
   Tell him I'm flying, yeh, tell him I'm flying, yeh.

3. If he asks you, yeh, was I laughing, yeh . . .
   Tell him I'm crying, yeh, tell him I'm crying, yeh.

4. I don't want no, yeh, cornbread or molasses, yeh . . .
   They hurt my pride, yeh, they hurt my pride, yeh.

Old Smokey

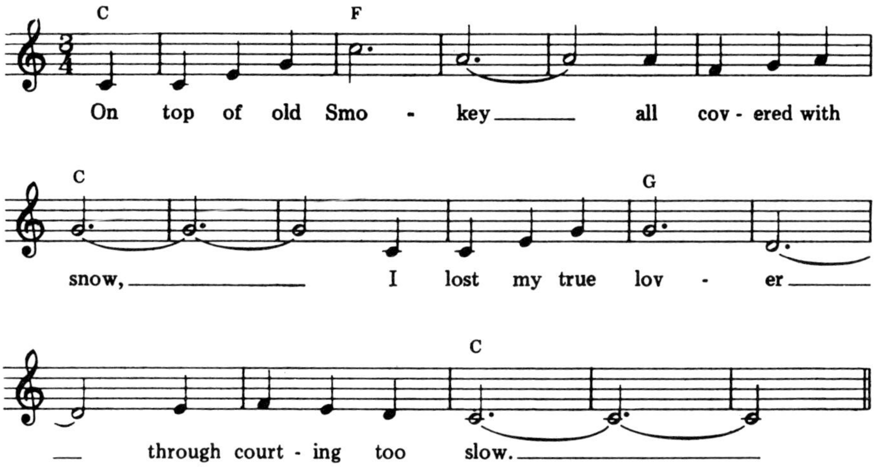

2. Now courting's a pleasure and parting is grief,
But a false hearted lover is worse than a thief.

3. A thief will just rob you and take all you save,
But a false hearted lover drives you to your grave.

4. And the grave will just rot you and turn you to dust,
Not a boy in ten million a poor girl can trust.

5. They'll hug you and kiss you and tell you more lies,
Than the cross-ties on a rail road or stars in the sky.

6. They tell you they love you to give your heart ease,
But the moment your back is turned they court who they please.

7. So come all you young maidens and listen to me,
Never hang your affections on a green willow tree.

8. For the leaves they will perish and the leaves they will die,
And you'll be forsaken and you'll never know why.

One more river to cross

2. The animals went in one by one,
   There's one more river to cross,
   The elephant eating a currant bun,
   There's one more river to cross.

3. The animals went in two by two,
   The elephant and the kangaroo,

4. The animals went in three by three,
   The bear, the flea and the bumble-bee,

5. The animals went in four by four,
   The hippopotamus got stuck in the door,

6. The animals went in five by five,
   Some were dead and some alive,

7. The animals went in six by six,
   The hyena laughed at the monkey's tricks,

8. The animals went in seven by seven,
   Said the ant to the elephant 'Who is you shovin'?',

9. The animals went in eight by eight,
   Some were early and some were late,

10. The animals went in nine by nine,
    Said the whale: 'Not me, the water's fine',

11. The animals went in ten by ten,
    The ark she blowed her whistle then,

12. And then the voyage did begin,
    Old Noah pulled the gang-plank in,

13. They never knew where they were at,
    Till the old ark bumped on Ararat,

14. The old ark landed high and dry,
    The baboon kissed the cow goodbye.

Oh, me taters and me 'ot fried fish

An unusual Cockney song which should, of course, be sung in a Cockney accent!

Ain't you glad

2. In the book.

3. In the blood.

4. Over yonder.

5. All you sinners.

6. All the good uns.

7. Now I'm glad.

8. So ain't you glad?

Travel on

2. Mary writes to Johnny, Johnny can't write home,
   Johnny can't write home, Johnny can't write home,
   Mary writes to Johnny, Johnny can't write home,
   'Cos he feels that he's gotta travel on.

3. I want to see my honey, want to see her bad . . .
   She's the best gal this poor guy's ever had.

4. High Sheriff and police are coming after me . . .
   So I feel like I've got to travel on.

5. I see that train a coming, coming round the bend . . .
   And I know that I've got to travel on.

My Lord, what a morning

2. Gonna meet all my brothers . . .
3. Gonna read the Holy Bible,
4. Gonna meet my blessed Jesus,
5. Gonna sing those glorious old songs,

My Lord, what a morning–New version

Chorus

My Lord, what a morning,
My Lord, what a morning,
My Lord, what a morning,
On that Christmas tide.

1. Turned away from the village inn,
2. Made their way to a stable,
3. Jesus born in that stable,
4. He was laid in a manger,
5. Stable beasts for companions,
6. Shepherds came and gazed in wonder,
7. Wise men travelled to adore Him,
8. Brought their gifts to lay before Him,
9. So the King of Kings joined us.

We're all together again, we're here

This verse should be sung several times using different accents: Scottish, yokel, BBC announcer, vicar, etc.

Sinner man

2. Run to the sea, sea will be a boiling,
   Run to the sea, sea will be a boiling,
   Run to the sea, sea will be a boiling,
   All on that day.

3. Run to the stars, stars will be a falling,

4. Run to the moon, moon will be a bleeding,

5. Run to the rocks, rocks won't you hide me?

6. Run to the devil, devil won't you hide me?

7. Run to the Lord, Lord won't you save me?

8. Run to the sea, sea will be a boiling,
   Run to the stars, stars will be a falling,
   Run to the moon, moon will be a bleeding,
   All on that day.

Hey lilley, lilley, lilley

2. Two old ladies sitting in the sand,
   Hey lilley, lilley, oh,
   Each one wishing that the other was a man,
   Hey lilley, lilley, oh.

3. Will you listen to my thesis,
   Peace in the world or the world in pieces.

4. There's many more verses to this song,
   You can make them up as you go along.

What shall we do with the drunken sailor?

2. Take him, shake him, try to wake him,
3. Give him lashings with a rope end,
4. Bathe his wounds with salty water,
5. Sling him in the long boat till he's sober,
6. Pull out the plug and wet him all over,
7. Put him below until he's sober,

8. Get a hose and wet him all over,

9. Shave his tummy with a rusty razor,

10. Send him up the crow's nest until he falls down.

11. Tie him to the taffrail when she's yardarm under,

12. That's what we'll do with the drunken sailor.

After the ball was over

A well known song but with unusual words!

The Fox

2. Well he ran till he came to a great big pen,
   Where the ducks and the geese were kept therein,
   He said 'A couple of you's going to grease my chin,
   Before I leave this town-o . . .'

3. He grabbed the grey goose by the neck,
   And he swung the duck up on his back,
   He didn't mind the quack, quack, quack,
   And the legs all dangling down-o . . .

4. Well old Mother Flipper Flopper jumped out of bed,
   Threw back the shutters and stuck out her head,
   Cried 'John, John! the grey goose is gone,
   And the fox is on the town-o . . .'

5. John he ran to the top of the hill,
   And blew his little horn both loud and shrill,
   The fox said 'I'd better flee with my kill,
   For they'll soon be on my trail-o . . .'

6. He ran till he came to his cozy little den,
   There sat the little ones eight, nine, ten,
   They said 'Daddy better go back again,
   For it must be a mighty fine town-o . . .'

7. The fox and his wife without any strife,
   Cut up the goose with a fork and a knife,
   They never had such a supper in their lives,
   And the little ones chewed on the bones-o . . .

Deep blue sea

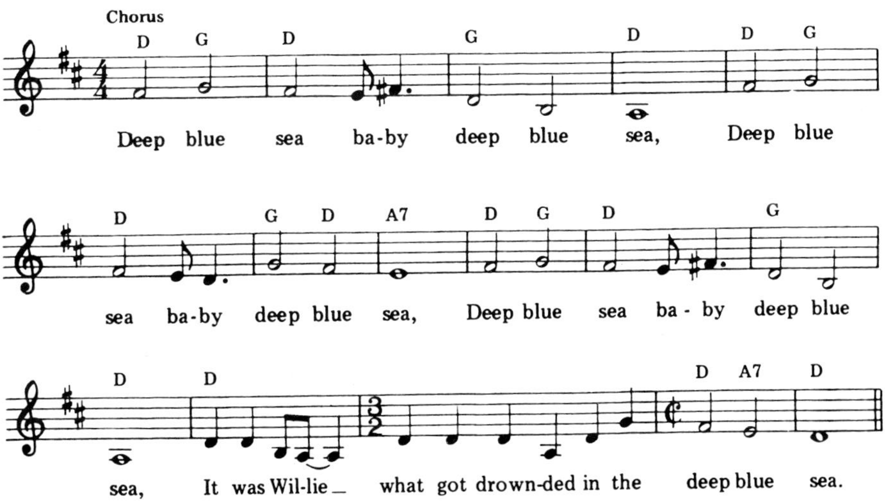

2. Dig his grave with a silver spade,
   Dig his grave with a silver spade,
   Dig his grave with a silver spade,
   It was Willie what got drownded
   In the deep blue sea.

3. Wrap his body in a silken shroud,

4. Lower him down with a golden chain,

5. Golden sun bring him back to me.

Oh, hand me down my walking cane

1. Oh, hand me down my old six gun,
   Oh, hand me down my old six gun,
   Oh, hand me down my old six gun,
   I'll make them coyotes run,
   All my sins are taken away.
2. Oh, hand me down my bottle of corn,
   Get drunk and roll on the floor.
3. Oh, hand me down my old guitar,
   I'll play it near and far.
4. Oh, hand me down my old banjo,
   I'll play it fast and slow.
5. Now the beans are hard and the meat is fat,
   I couldn't eat any of that.
6. Now I got caught and put in jail,
   And no one would go my bail.
7. If I had listened to what Mama said,
   I'd been sleeping on a feather bed.

I'm so glad

2. I'm so glad there's a meeting here tonight,
   I'm so glad there's a meeting here tonight,
   I'm so glad there's a meeting here tonight,
   Sing glory hallelujah,
   I'm so glad.

3. I'm so glad we're brothers everyone,

4. I'm so glad we're fighting to be free,

5. I'm so glad we're travelling life's road,

6. I'm so glad we're happy everyone,

7. I'm so glad we're singing here tonight.

Bog down in the valley, O

2. And on this tree there was a bough,
   Rare bough, a rattling bough,
   And the bough on the tree,
   And the tree in the bog,
   And the bog down in the valley, o.

3. And on this bough there was a branch,
   Rare branch, a rattling branch,
   And the branch on the bough,
   And the bough on the tree,
   And the tree in the bog,
   And the bog down in the valley, o.

4. And on this branch there was a twig,

5. And on this twig there was a nest,

6. And in this nest there was an egg,

7. And on this egg there was a bird,

8. And then this bird she flew away, Aaahh!
Rare bird, a rattling bird,
And the bird left the egg,
And the egg in the nest,
And the nest on the twig,
And the twig on the branch,
And the branch on the bough,
And the bough on the tree,
And the tree in the bog,
And the bog down in the valley, o.

Daisy, Daisy

2. Michael, Michael, this is my answer, dear,
I can't cycle, it makes me feel so queer,
If you can't afford a carriage,
Bang goes this blinking marriage,
'Cos I'll be blowed if I'll be towed
On a bicycle built for two!

Down by the riverside

xx - claps

2. Gonna put on my long white robe.

3. Gonna lay down my sword and shield.

4. Gonna ride in the golden chariot.

5. Gonna try on my silver crown.

6. Gonna climb the road to Heaven.

7. I'll fight the wicked devil.

8. Gonna climb upon that mountain.

9. Gonna cross the river of Jordan.

10. Gonna read the Holy Bible.

11. Gonna meet my blessed Jesus.

Closing Songs

Over the years a number of songs have become recognised as closing songs – occasionally a new one comes along which fits straight into this slot but most have been closing songs for years.

These songs, properly treated, should put your audience in a thoughtful mood which will be enhanced if you choose your closing prayer carefully.

Going down the valley

This song could almost have been written for bringing a camp fire to a close. An effective touch is to ask everyone to stand then start this song, as you sing the first verse for the third time gradually swing your arm round the circle indicating the audience to sit, then you sing the second verse for the third time you swing your arm back around the circle so that they all stand again.

This should be sung three times.

We are coming up the valley,
Coming up the valley,
Coming up the valley, one by one, one by one,
We are coming up the valley,
Coming up the valley,
Coming to the rising of the sun.

This should also be sung three times.

Land of the silver birch

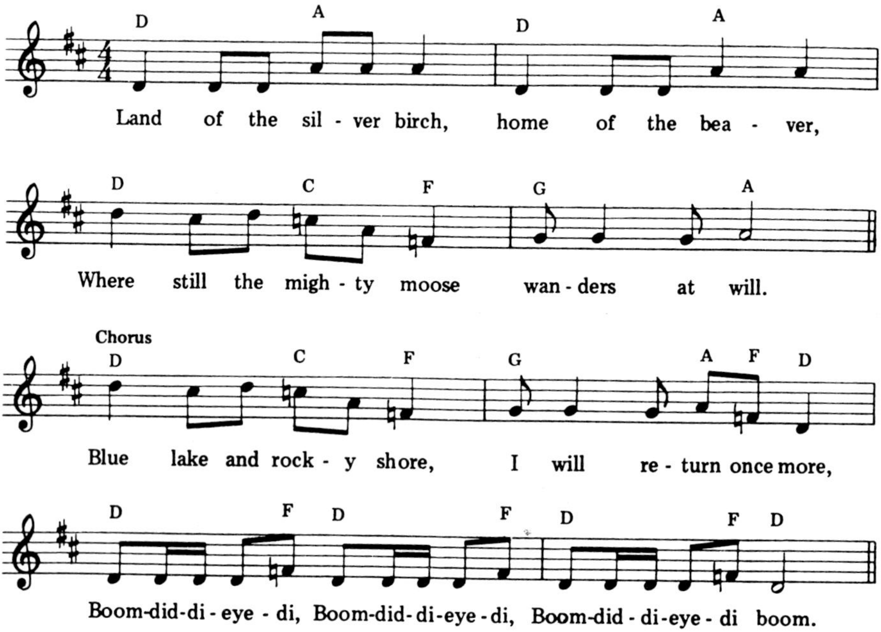

2. My heart is sick for you,
   Here in the lowlands,
   I will return to you,
   Hills of the north.

3. Swift as the silver fish,
   Canoe of birch bark,
   Thy mighty waters,
   Carry me forth.

4. There where the blue lake lies,
   I'll set my wigwam,
   Close to the water's edge,
   Silent and still.

Kum ba yah

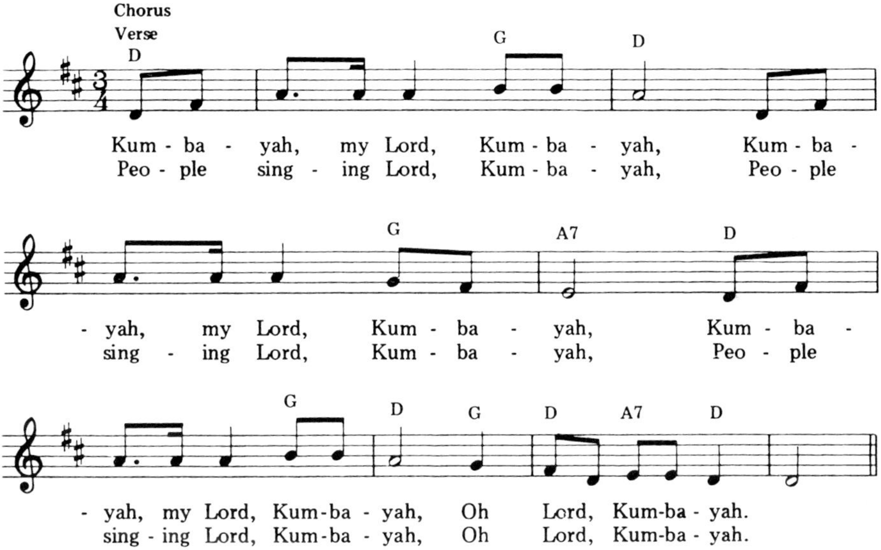

2. We are happy Lord, kum ba yah.

3. Children playing Lord, kum ba yah.

4. Nations fighting Lord, kum ba yah.

5 Mothers weeping Lord, kum ba yah.

6. Families mourning Lord, kum ba yah.

7. Why this fighting Lord? kum ba yah.

8. Peace in our time Lord, kum ba yah.

9. So we're praying Lord, kum ba yah.

Gloria, gloria, gloria

This is a beautiful song which should be sung well or not at all. It is a Latin verse meaning 'Glory to God on high'.

It is really a three part round, each part has the same words but each is sung differently.

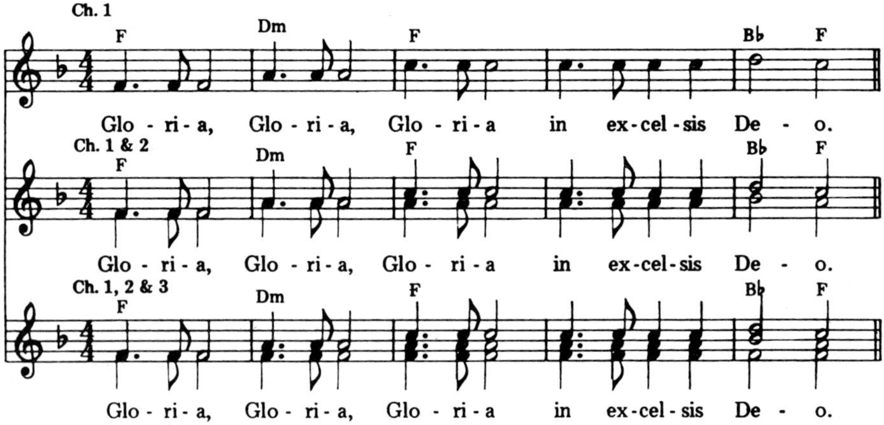

Day is done, gone the sun (Taps)

This song is frequently used as the final song of the fire. It should be sung very quietly to give maximum effect.

It can also be sung in the daytime, with the following words:

Thanks and praise for our days
'Neath the sun, 'neath the stars, 'neath the sky.
As we go, this we know.
God is nigh.

Rock my soul

2. Too wide, can't get round it,
   Too wide, can't get round it,
   Too wide, can't get round it,
   Got to go through the door, O Lordy.

3. Too deep, can't get under it,

4. Too high, can't get over it,
   Too wide, can't get round it,
   Too deep, can't get under it,
   Got to go through the door, O Lordy.

Goodnight ladies

This is another excellent song to end a fire – it is also a nice way to say Goodnight to your audience and participants.

2. Goodnight Cub Scouts,

3. Goodnight Scouts,

4. Goodnight Guides,
   etc.

Resource Material

As we said in the introduction, this book can only contain a mere fraction of all the thousands of songs that could have been included. Set out below are a few ideas and addresses which may help you in your searches for new material or, indeed, for the words or music to something that you have heard or played but have never been able to trace.

The Scout Association Books

Camp Fire Books – *The Scout Song Book*
The Hackney Scout Song Book
Scout Pops
Folk Books – *Bangor Song Book*

The Girl Guides Association Books

The Girl Guide Song Books 1 *& 2; 36pp.*

Other Publisher's Books

The Penguin Book of English Folk Songs: 128pp.; ISBN 0 14 70818 9

Cub Scout Songs by Brian Sims, (Brown, Son & Ferguson, Ltd.; 66pp.)

I'll Sing You One, Oh (The English Folk Dance & Song Society: 70pp. ISBN 084518 019 2.)

Prayer Books

Scout Prayers (The Scout Association; 64pp. ISBN 0 85165 168 2.)

Prayers for Young People by William Barclay (Fontana (Religious); 96pp. ISBN 0 00 6245 80 3.)

Interrobang by Norman C. Hable (Lutterworth Press; 96pp. SBN 7188 1760 5.)

Sheet Music – The English Folk Dance and Song Society has very extensive libraries covering most folk songs and they willingly supply sheet music, or, if unobtainable, photostat copies, upon request.

Records and Tapes – These appear under all sorts of record labels so regular visits to your record shop are the best way of keeping your collection up to date. The Topic Record Company specialises in producing folk records and these are well worth looking out for.

Useful Addresses

Folk enquiries
The English Folk Dance and Song Society,
Cecil Sharp House,
2 Regent's Park Road,
London NW1 7AY.

Camp Fire enquiries
The Warden,
Gilwell Park National Scout Camp Site,
Chingford,
London E4 7QW.

Book Suppliers

Scout Shops Ltd, on sale at all shops or direct from
Scout Shops Ltd,
Churchill Industrial Estate,
Lancing,
West Sussex BN15 8UG.

The Scout and Guides Club,
U.C.N.W. Students Union,
Bangor,
North Wales.

The Girl Guides Association,
17–19 Buckingham Palace Road,
London SW1W 0PT.

The English Folk Dance and Song Society,
Address given above.

Chords

Here are most of the chords you will need to play the songs in this book. An asterisk denotes a string that should not be struck.

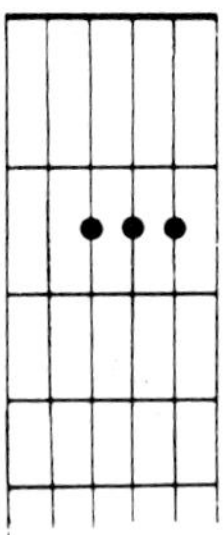

A

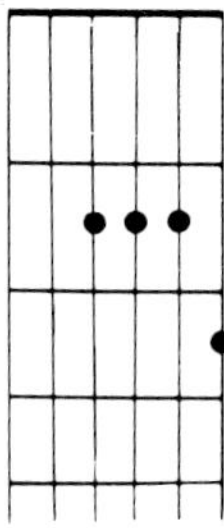

A7

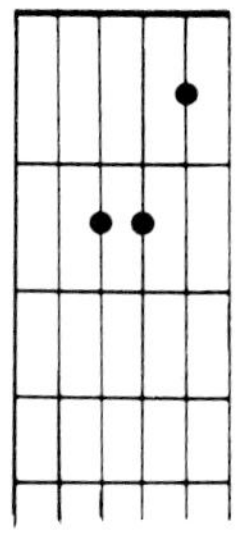

Am

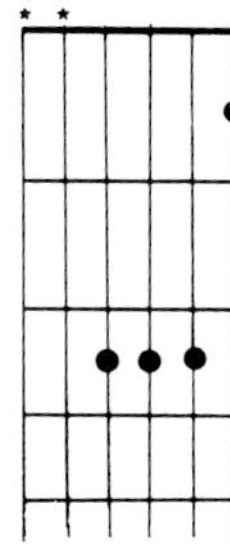

B♭

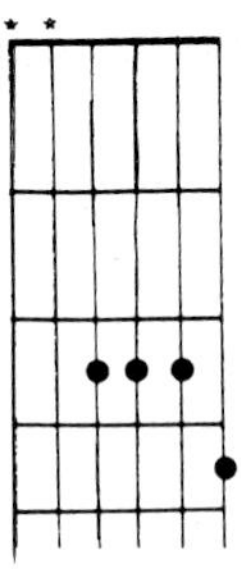

B♭7

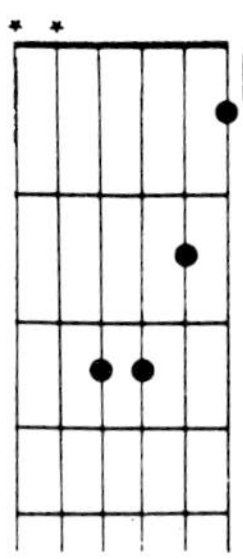

B♭m

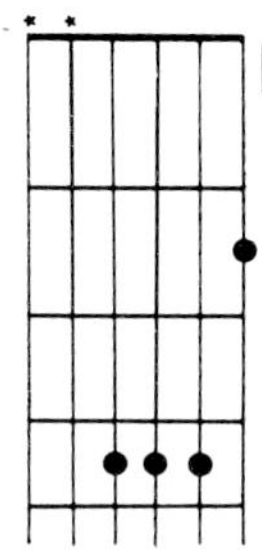

B

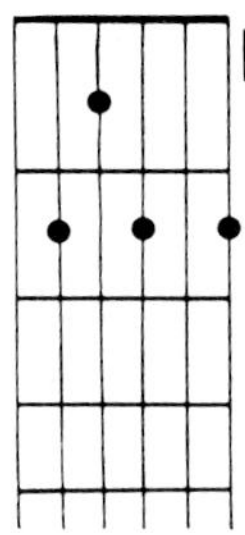

B7

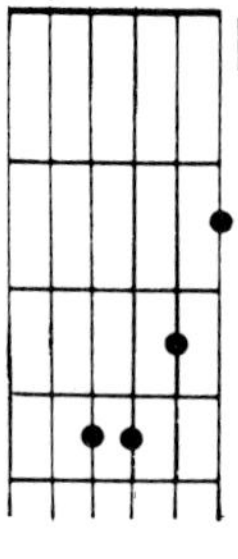

Bm

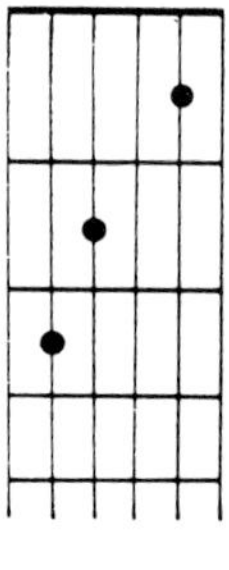

C

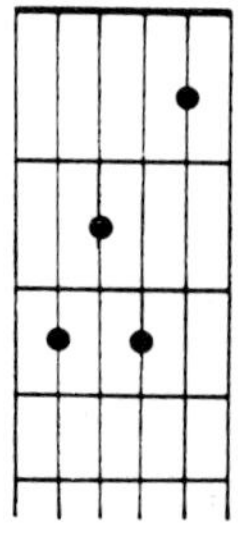

C7

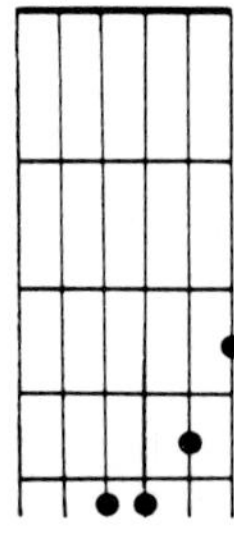

Cm

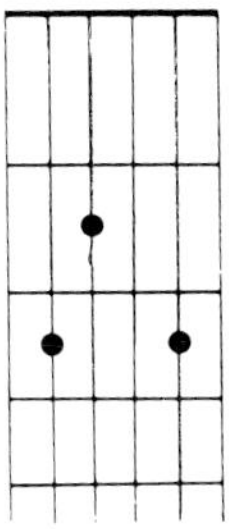
C9

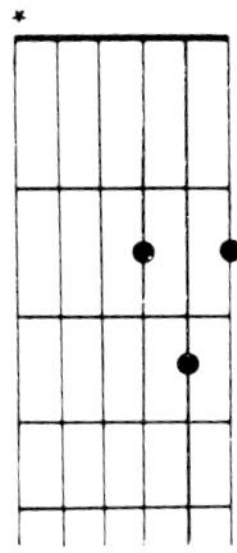
D

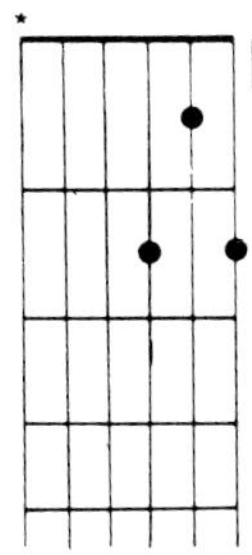
D7

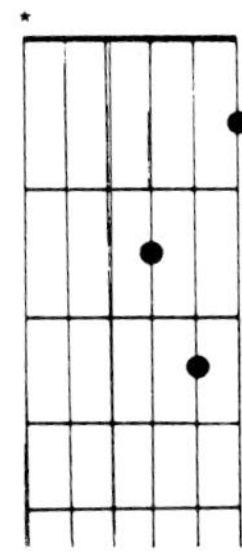
Dm

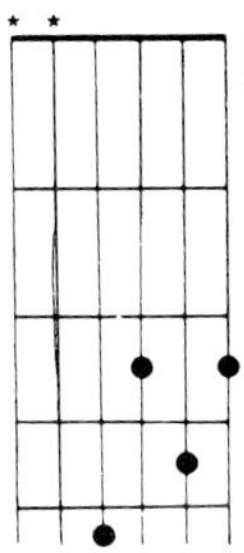
E♭

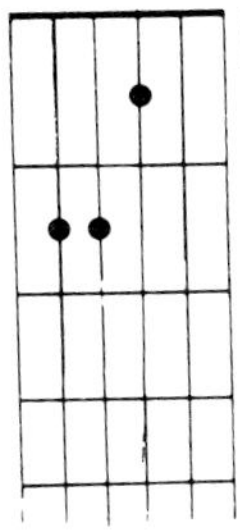
E

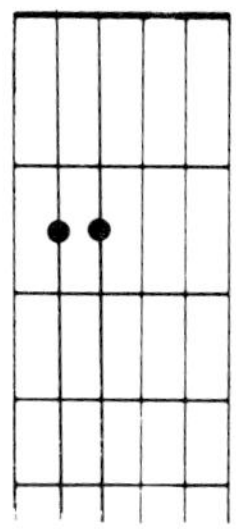
Em

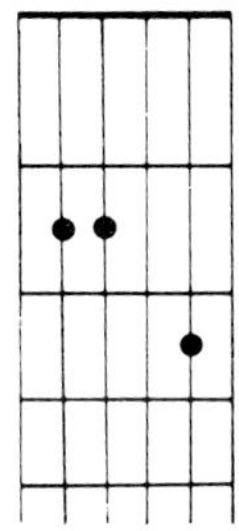
Em7

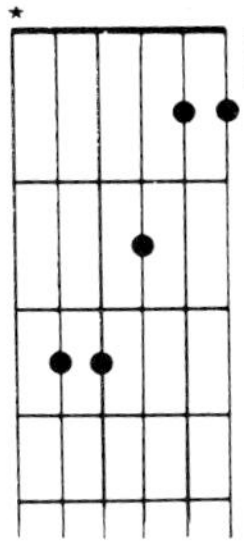
F

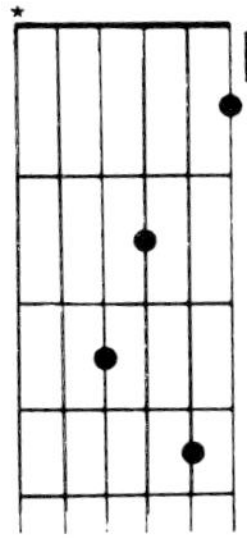
F7

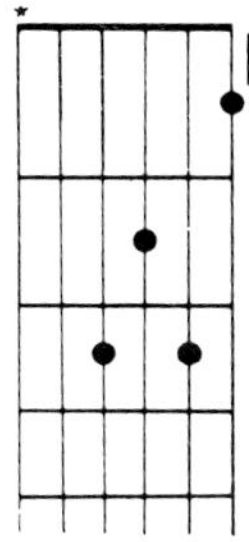
F6

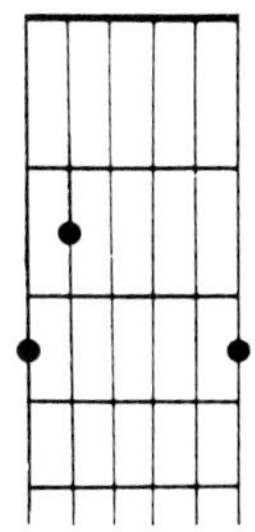
G

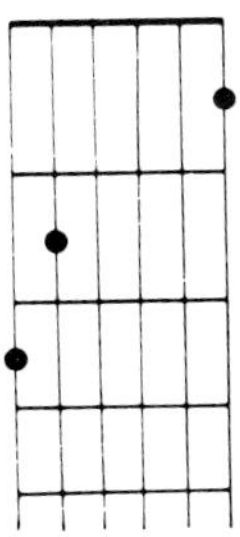
G7

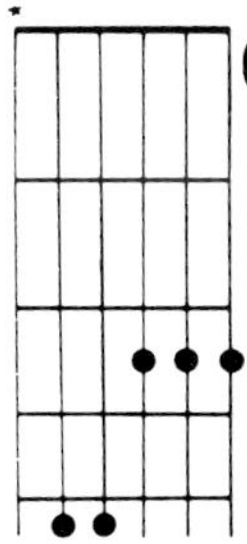
Gm

Index